SEE-THROUGH
MUMMIES

John Malam

RUNNING PRESS
KIDS

Library of Congress
Control Number: 2002095723

ISBN 13: 978-0-7624-1586-1
ISBN 10: 0-7624-1586-X

This book was created by
THE ILEX PRESS LTD
Cambridge CB2 4LX

PUBLISHER Alastair Campbell
EXECUTIVE PUBLISHER Sophie Collins
CREATIVE DIRECTOR Peter Bridgewater
EDITORIAL DIRECTOR Steve Luck
DESIGN MANAGER Tony Seddon
SENIOR PROJECT EDITOR Caroline Earle
DESIGNER Kevin Knight
ILLUSTRATIONS Julian Baker

This book may be ordered by mail from the
publisher. Please include $2.50 for postage and
handling. But try your bookstore first!

Running Press Book Publishers
125 South Twenty-second Street
Philadelphia, Pennsylvania 19103-4399

Visit us on the web!
www.runningpress.com

To contact the author, write to:
johnmalam@aol.com

CONTENTS

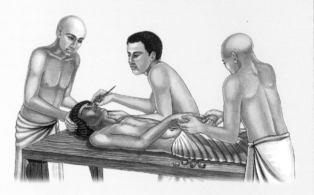

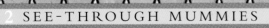

ANCIENT EGYPT'S FIRST MUMMIES

Egypt is a hot, dry country in North Africa, and its climate has played an important role throughout its long history. In one very special way the country's natural conditions seem to have given the ancient Egyptians the idea for a practice for which they are well known today—the craft of mummification. The Egyptians were not the first to preserve, or mummify, the bodies of dead people—that claim to fame belongs to the inhabitants of northern Chile, who made mummies 2,000 years before the Egyptians ever did. However, in the skilled hands of Egyptian embalmers, the dead bodies of people and animals were saved from rotting away, and these became the most famous mummies of all time.

NATURE'S MUMMIES

Egypt's first mummies were made by nature. They date from around 3500 BCE. A dead person was buried in a pit scooped in the sandy ground. Because the sand was hot and dry, the body dried out. It shriveled and its skin became tightly stretched over its skeleton. During the course of many years, the body slowly turned into a natural mummy.

Pit burial   Weathered mound   Grave discovered

△ **From man to mummy**
A body is buried in a pit and the grave is covered with sand. Time passes. The grave is forgotten and the body mummifies. Finally, the grave is found. Inside the grave is a natural mummy.

BODY IN THE SAND

As years passed, people forgot where a body was buried. The mound of sand over the grave weathered and became flat. When the grave was found, perhaps by robbers intent on stealing the grave goods, instead of finding a skeleton, they saw a naturally mummified body.

A last farewell ▽
After prayers were said and goods for the next life were placed beside the body, the grave was filled with sand, and the body disappeared from sight.

A priest may have spoken a few prayers at the graveside.

The body was laid to rest on its side. The dead person looked as if he were lying down to sleep.

Grave goods

The dead person's arms were held to his chest, and his legs, bent at the knees, were tucked under it.

◁ **Grave goods**
From the earliest times, Egypt's dead were buried with grave goods—items for use in the next life. There were pots of food and drink, flint knives, beads, and stone palettes on which eye paint was mixed.

Stone palette

THE EGYPTIAN AFTERLIFE

Egypt's first artificial mummies were made around 3400 BCE. These mummies were deliberately made. Unlike the older natural mummies, which were accidents of nature, there was nothing accidental about an artificial mummy. It was made by skilled workers called embalmers, whose job was to preserve a body and stop it from rotting away. Human bodies were mummified because the Egyptians believed their "owners" still needed them after they died. To the Egyptian way of thinking, death was not the end of a person's life. Rather, it was another stage in a person's life cycle. They thought of death as a change from one form of existence to another. In the words of the Egyptians themselves, death was the "night of going forth to life."

TO LIVE FOREVER

The Egyptians believed that people could live forever after they had died. However, everlasting life was possible only if certain essential requirements were carried out. The most important requirement was for the dead person's body to be preserved, since, as a mummy, it would act as a shelter for various spirits while the person made the difficult journey to the next life. Every Egyptian wanted to be reborn in the afterlife, and the rituals that took place between death and burial were designed to make this desire come true.

Members of the family paid their last respects to the dead person.

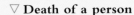
▽ Death of a person
When someone died, it marked a time of sadness and mourning for their family. Preparations soon began for the person's embalming and funeral.

Women mourners cried out, pulled their hair, and beat their chests in grief.

Priests, such as this sem-priest dressed in a leopardskin robe, offered prayers for the dead person.

MUMMY MATTERS

 How and when were mummies made?

- The word "mummy" is from the Arabic word *mummiya*, meaning bitumen—a type of black tar, which was smeared onto some mummies.
- Mummies were made in Egypt for about 3,800 years.
- The last Egyptian mummies were made around 400 CE.
- At different times in Egyptian history, different methods were used to make mummies.

△ A person's ba
The *ba*, pictured as a bird with a human head, was the personality or unique character of a person. It ate, spoke, and visited the realm of the living.

△ A person's ka
The *ka*, pictured as a pair of upstretched arms, was a person's vital or life force. It was their exact double. After death, the *ka* lived within the person's mummy.

△ A person's akh
The *akh*, pictured as a crested ibis, formed when the *ba* joined the *ka* in the afterlife. Only then was the person reborn—he or she had reached the state of "*akh*."

◁ **Field of Reeds**
The Egyptian idea of heaven was a place where fields of giant wheat grew, where no one was hungry, and where everyone was happy all the time. This paradise was called the Field of Reeds. It was where people hoped to live forever in a new life after death.

Akh bird

BODY, SPIRITS, PERSON

The ancient Egyptians had a very different way of thinking about the "parts" that made a person. Most people today think of themselves as divided into a body and a soul. The ancient Egyptians thought they were made up of a body, together with five different parts, or spirit forms. The three main spirits were the *ba*, the *ka*, and the all-important *akh* (the "shadow" and the "name" were the other two parts). After a person was buried, the *ba* and the *ka* lived in the tomb where they attended to the person's needs. The *ba* was free to come and go as it wished, while the *ka* was more restricted in its movements—it lived within the mummy. For the person to be reborn and live in the afterlife, the *ba* and the *ka* had to join together, at which point the person's *akh* was created. Every Egyptian wanted to "become *akh*" after death—only then would he or she be immortal.

Priests attended to the body of a dead person, offering spells and prayers, and preparing it for the embalming process.

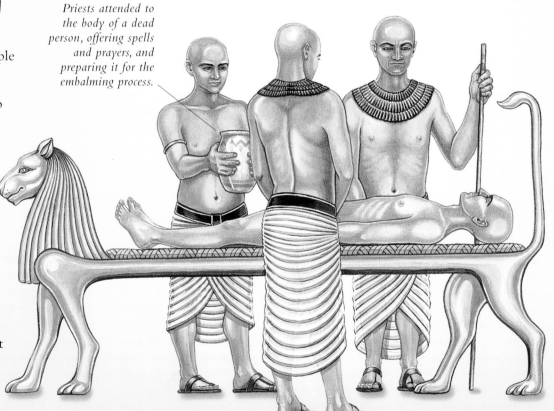

ROUTE TO THE NEXT LIFE

When people died they didn't begin their new existence in the afterlife right away. Instead, the Egyptians believed a dead person had to make a journey from this world to the next. There was no direct route or short cut to the afterlife. Everyone, from commoner to pharaoh, had to travel along fixed routes, which took them across rivers and fiery lakes, past hostile creatures, and through closed gates. Only if the person knew the correct words and spells to say, and passed certain tests, would he or she be allowed to enter the next life, or Field of Reeds.

◁ **Arrival of the embalmers**
Soon after a person died, the embalmers were called in by the family. The dead body was entrusted to the embalmers, and they took it away to their place of work.

OSIRIS—EGYPT'S FIRST MUMMY

The ancient Egyptians had many gods and goddesses. They told stories about them, putting into words things that were difficult to understand. One of their greatest stories was about how the very first mummy came to be made. The story was a way of explaining the reasons why mummies were made, and because it involved one of Egypt's most important gods, people wanted to be mummified just like him when they died. His name was Osiris, and he was Egypt's first mummy.

▽ **Perfect fit**
Seth made the coffin in the shape of Osiris and promised to give it to the man it fitted, which is how he tricked Osiris to lie inside it.

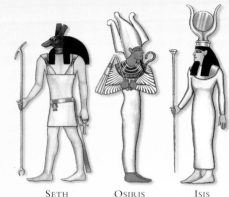

△ **Osiris's brother and sister**
Osiris was shown in white, to represent the wrappings of a mummy. He was married to his sister, Isis, and had an evil brother, Seth.

Seth   Osiris   Isis

THE DEATH OF OSIRIS

Osiris, god of death and rebirth, had a sister, Isis, and a brother, Seth. Isis was kind and loving, but Seth was evil. Osiris was loved by the people of Egypt. Seth grew jealous of his brother, and tricked him to lie down inside a box. The box was a coffin. Seth shut the lid and threw the coffin into the Nile River, and Osiris drowned. The coffin floated far away. Isis searched for Osiris, and when she found his body she brought it home to Egypt and hid it. Then, one day, Seth found the body of Osiris. He was angry that Osiris had returned, and he ripped his body into fourteen pieces, which he scattered across Egypt. That, surely, would be the end of Osiris, thought Seth.

MUMMY MATTERS

 Osiris, the "eternally good being"

- Because he was the first mummy, Osiris was also thought of as the first person to survive death and live again in the next life.
- Artists often pictured Osiris with green skin. Green was the color of new life, since it was the color of the plants that grew from the black mud of farmers' fields. Green stood for being born again.
- People thought Osiris brought civilization and agriculture to Egypt, which is why he was so important to them. They called him the "eternally good being."

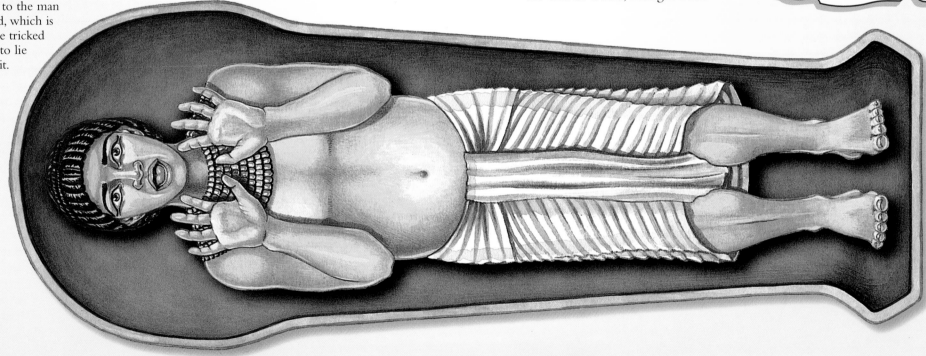

ISIS FINDS THE PIECES

When Isis discovered what Seth had done, she was filled with a terrible sadness. She could not bear to think of Osiris lying in pieces across Egypt, so she took it upon herself to find them. Isis became a kite (a bird of prey), and as she looked down upon the land, she could see where Seth had hidden the body parts of Osiris. She found them all save one, which a great fish had swallowed. Isis brought the pieces together in one place, and hoped a miracle would happen. But she did not have the magic to bring her dead brother back to life. She wept. Isis needed help.

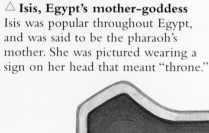

△ **Isis, Egypt's mother-goddess**
Isis was popular throughout Egypt, and was said to be the pharaoh's mother. She was pictured wearing a sign on her head that meant "throne."

Jackal head

OSIRIS IS REBORN

When Ra, the sun god, saw Isis crying, he sent two gods to help her—Anubis, the god of embalming, and Thoth, the god of wisdom. Anubis took each piece of Osiris's body, anointed it with oils, and wrapped it in bandages. Isis, Anubis, and Thoth laid the pieces out in the shape of Osiris, and Anubis then wrapped the whole body. The first mummy was made. Isis blew life into Osiris and he was reborn, not to live in this world, but to live for all time in the afterlife, where he would be the king of the dead.

Jackal-headed Anubis △
Anubis, pictured as a jackal or a man with the head of a jackal, had a black face. Black was the color of life, since Egypt's black soil gave birth to plants.

THOTH

Wrapped for all eternity ▽
The Osiris story was a promise. People believed that if their bodies were mummified, then they, too, would live forever in the afterlife, just like Osiris did.

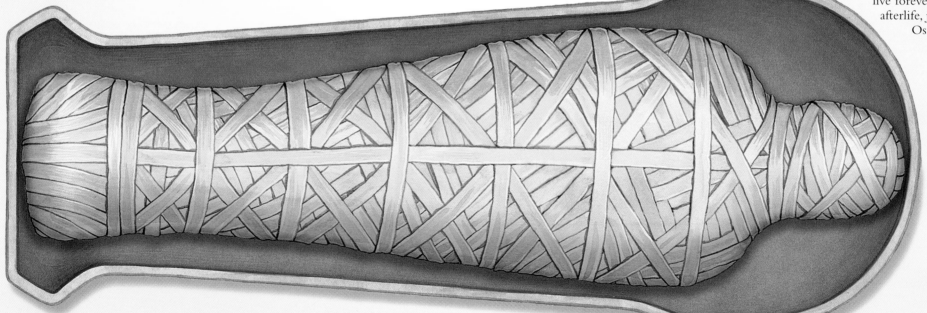

ANCIENT EGYPT'S MUMMY MAKERS

It was during the period of ancient Egyptian history known as the New Kingdom (about 1550–1069 BCE) that Egypt's embalmers produced the finest and most elaborate mummies. This was the time when the craft of mummy-making was at its best. The mummification process described on the following pages is based on how a New Kingdom mummy was made. It was a long, slow process, and, if the correct procedures were all carried out, it usually took seventy days to transform a flesh-and-blood dead body into a dried-out mummy. The mummification process took place inside several open-air tents, which were makeshift structures of reeds and matting. They were close to water, and never far from where the mummy was to be buried.

Only men worked inside the embalmers' workshop tents.

PLACE OF PURIFICATION

After a person died, embalmers collected the body. They placed it in a wooden coffin, which they put onto a sledge, or bier, and took it to the Nile River. From there, the coffin was taken by boat to the west bank of the river. Once ashore, the coffin was taken to an embalmers' tent called the "Place of Purification" (*ibu* in ancient Egyptian), where the body was washed with a solution of natron (a type of salt). This purified the body, and only then was it ready to be mummified.

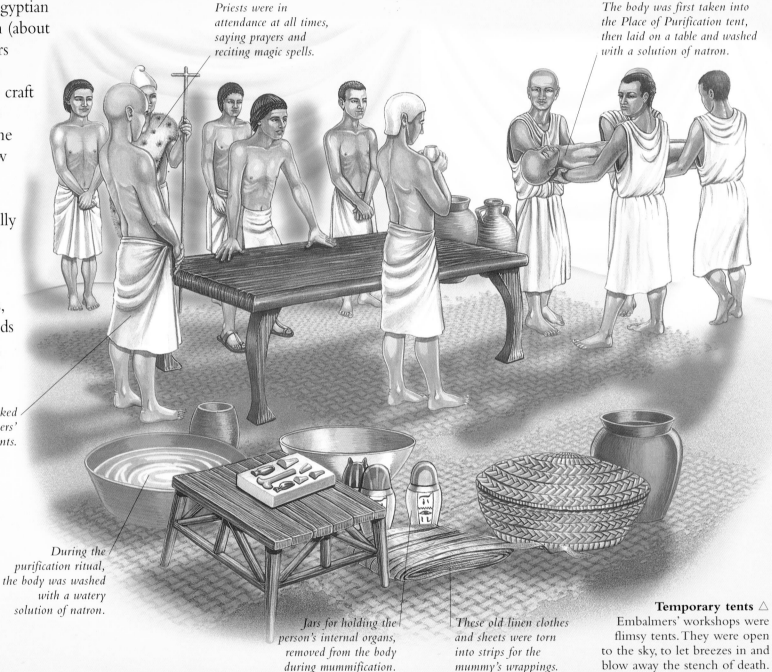

Priests were in attendance at all times, saying prayers and reciting magic spells.

The body was first taken into the Place of Purification tent, then laid on a table and washed with a solution of natron.

During the purification ritual, the body was washed with a watery solution of natron.

Jars for holding the person's internal organs, removed from the body during mummification.

These old linen clothes and sheets were torn into strips for the mummy's wrappings.

Temporary tents △
Embalmers' workshops were flimsy tents. They were open to the sky, to let breezes in and blow away the stench of death.

A FAMILY BUSINESS

As with other jobs in ancient Egypt, from baker to jeweler, priest to scribe, the craft of embalming was a family business. Embalmers were only ever men, and their jobs were passed from father to son. It was a father's duty to train his son to become an embalmer, just like he was. Families of embalmers worked together.

▽ **Like father, like son**
By watching his father and grandfather at work, a boy learned how to become an embalmer just like them.

GRANDFATHER

GRANDSON

FATHER

Embalmers' workshops.

◁ **Feeding the people**
Farmers were valued members of society, since they grew food to feed the people. Their main cereal crop was emmer (a primitive kind of wheat).

NILE, THE RIVER OF LIFE

The Nile River flows north through Egypt to the Mediterranean Sea. In ancient Egyptian times, it flooded every summer, dumping a layer of rich, black mud across its floodplain. When the flood went down, farmers grew crops in the fertile soil. Embalmers also needed the Nile for their work, since it provided them with water to wash bodies. To them, water had life-giving qualities— it was a symbol of rebirth. By washing a body before mummifying it, they were preparing it to be reborn.

Person's name

△ **Buried with the mummy**
Spells from the Book of the Dead, written on a papyrus scroll, were buried with the mummy. The person's name was written into the spells, to protect him or her on the journey to the afterlife.

BOOK OF SPELLS

While the embalmers worked, a priest recited sacred words from the Book of the Dead. This was a collection of around two hundred spells, all of which were designed to help the dead person travel to the afterlife. The spells were believed to be powerful magic.

EGYPTIAN CEMETERIES

Embalmers worked close to the cemetery where a mummy was to be buried. Over the centuries, different types of cemeteries were used. The pyramids at Giza, near Cairo, were a cemetery for Egypt's first pharaohs. Later rulers were buried in valley cemeteries, in tombs cut into the rock. Nobles and commoners were often buried in underground tombs, as at the massive cemetery at Saqqara, near Cairo, which was in use for more than 3,000 years.

City of the dead △
Only after a mummy had been sealed inside its tomb in a cemetery, or necropolis (a Greek word meaning "city of the dead"), could the dead person begin the journey to the afterlife.

REMOVING THE BODY'S ORGANS

After the body had been ritually cleansed in the "Place of Purification" tent, it was taken out and carried over to the "House of Beauty" (*per-nefer* in ancient Egyptian). This was the tent where embalmers performed the actual process of mummification. The naked body was placed on its back on a flat embalming table. The table was not level with the ground, but had a slight slope. The slope allowed liquid to run off the table and fall to the ground, where it was caught in a bowl. The head of the body was always at the table's higher end. The team of embalmers worked around the table, and each man had a specific job to do.

WHY TAKE ORGANS OUT?

Embalmers began the mummification process by opening the body and removing most of its internal organs. They did this quickly, and as soon after death as possible. If the organs were not removed, or if they were left in the body too long, they would start to decompose and destroy the body.

THE EMBALMERS' TOOL KIT

Embalmers used simple tools. Knives for cutting through flesh were made from razor-sharp stones, such as flint and obsidian (a type of glasslike volcanic rock). Metal hooks and spoons helped remove the organs, and wads of linen soaked up body fluids. The most effective tools an embalmer used were his own bare hands.

The chief embalmer wore a jackal mask, to symbolize the animal's link with the dead.

The slitter made a cut in the left side of the abdomen, pushed his hands inside, and pulled out the lungs, liver, intestines, and stomach. The heart and kidneys were left in the body.

The slitter passed the organs to the pickler, who took them away to be separately embalmed.

The Master of Secrets was the chief embalmer.

Removed organs were mummified, then placed in separate storage, or canopic, jars.

Embalming tables were quite low, and embalmers could sit or squat to do some of their work.

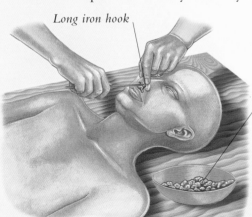

Long iron hook

Mashed brain

◁ **Removing the brain**
The brain was the first organ removed. It was pulled out in bits through the left nostril, or scooped through a hole at the base of the skull. It was thrown away and never preserved.

Teamwork △
Embalmers worked in a team. Each man had a specific job to do. They were fast workers, and it would not have taken long to remove the body's organs.

MUMMY MATTERS

Heart kept in, brain thrown away

- The Egyptians thought the heart, not the brain, was the center of a person's intelligence.
- The valuable heart was left in the body. The worthless brain was thrown away.
- The heart was needed to control the dead person in the next life.
- If the heart was accidentally removed, it was put back inside the body.

LIVER   LUNGS   STOMACH   INTESTINES

◁ **Preserving the organs**
In the same way that the body was embalmed, the removed organs were also preserved and made ready for burial with the mummy.

Team of workers ▽
The scribe drew a line on the body's side; the slitter cut down the line; the pickler took charge of the organs; the lector priest read sacred texts.

WASHED AGAIN

With the brain and other organs removed, the skull and body cavity were empty. The body looked hollow and bruised. Water was then used to thoroughly cleanse the body, washing it both inside and out. The dirty water was collected in storage pots. The body was then little more than an empty shell.

Water from the Nile River was used to wash the body.

The body cavity was washed out to remove anything that could rot and damage the mummification process.

Bowls and jars collected water and body fluids that drained from the embalming table.

Storage jar

△ **Washed with wine**
Water was not the only liquid a body could be washed with. One account says that bodies were also washed with wine made from the fruit of palm trees.

SCRIBE

SLITTER OR RIPPER-UP

PICKLER

LECTOR PRIEST

YOUR LIFE IN THEIR HANDS

Very little is known about the embalmers who carried out the mummification process. It's certain that they were highly respected members of Egyptian society, since the job of preparing a body for eternal life was, quite literally, in their hands. They, and they alone, knew how to make a mummy. It was their knowledge and skill that helped to preserve a body, which then made it possible for a dead person to be born again in the next life.

DRYING THE BODY

On the fifteenth day after death, following the removal of the body's internal organs and its final washing, the embalmers set about drying the body. Drying was the longest part of the mummification process and lasted about forty days. This was the time when the body's fluids were slowly but surely "sucked" out, transforming it from soft flesh to a hardened, shrunken shadow of its former self. To dry the body, embalmers used a type of divine salt they called *neteryt*, which meant "belonging to the god." We call it natron.

NATRON, SALT OF LIFE

North of Cairo is the Wadi Natrun, a valley with salt lakes. Each summer the lakes dried up, leaving a powdery white substance around their shores. This was natron, a salty mixture of sodium carbonate and sodium bicarbonate. Embalmers, and other workers, all had uses for it.

COVERED WITH NATRON

After the body cavity had been packed, and the empty skull had been filled with sawdust and wads of linen, the body was laid out on a bed of natron. Embalmers then covered it in a great heap of natron, leaving no flesh exposed. It took a huge amount of natron to dry a body, and more than 500 pounds (225 kg) was probably used.

Natron worked by slowly drawing every drop of moisture from the body until it was completely dehydrated.

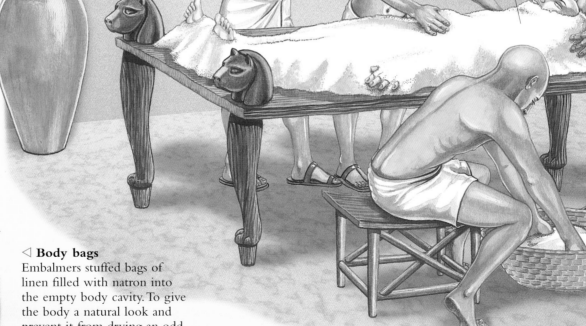

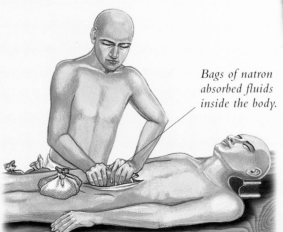

Bags of natron absorbed fluids inside the body.

◁ **Body bags**
Embalmers stuffed bags of linen filled with natron into the empty body cavity. To give the body a natural look and prevent it from drying an odd shape, rags, straw, dried grass, and sand were also put inside.

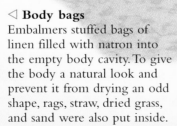

The dehydration experts △
Embalmers understood the drying properties of natron. Without it, they could not have made mummies.

FORTY DAYS OF DRYING

The body was left to dry out for forty days and forty nights. During this time, the embalmers may have checked it to "top up" the natron, and make sure no harm had come to it, especially from jackals, which might have tried to chew at it. Then, at the end of the drying-out time, the embalmers scraped away the natron to reveal the dried-out body. The natron had absorbed all its juices, and all body fat had completely disappeared.

PACKING THE BODY

After the drying-out process was over, embalmers began to restore the empty, shrivelled body to a lifelike appearance. They washed the body inside and out, then, when it was dry, packed it with bundles of linen, bags of natron, sawdust, mud, and anything else that came to hand—even onions!

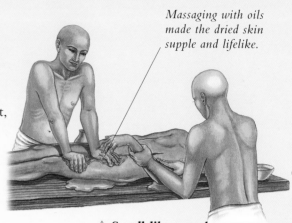

Massaging with oils made the dried skin supple and lifelike.

△ **Smell like a god**
It was thought that sweet-smelling oils made a body smell like a god.

ANOINTING THE BODY

After the body cavity had been packed, embalmers rubbed the skin with oils and perfumes. They used juniper oil, frankincense, myrrh, palm wine, and milk. Then, melted pine resin was poured over the body to stop it from going moldy.

△ **Drying the body's organs**
After being washed out, the intestines, lungs, liver, and stomach were placed in bowls and covered with natron. Just like the body, they, too, were dried out.

Body fluids that were not absorbed by the natron drained off the drying table.

The dried-out body was like a skeleton, covered with dark, wrinkled skin. Its limbs were like matchsticks.

The drying-out process made the body about seventy-five percent lighter.

△ **A long process**
By the time the body had dried out, about fifty-five days had elapsed since the person had died. There were still a further fifteen days to go before the person became a mummy.

The used bags of soggy natron and all other packing materials were taken from the body cavity. They were gathered up to be buried.

MUMMY MATTERS

 Long-distance trade in oil and resin

- Juniper oil was from Syria and Lebanon.
- Frankincense and myrrh were from Somalia and southern Arabia. They were tree resins (saps), dried into small red and yellow lumps.
- Ancient writers said cassia and cinnamon were used. They would have come from India and China.

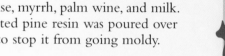

WRAPPING THE BODY

After drying, stuffing, and rubbing the body with oils, lifelike touches were added. Men were sometimes painted red (to make them look like they had been in the sun), while women's bodies were painted yellow (as if they had stayed pale in the shade). Women also had makeup applied—their eyebrows and lips were painted, and their cheeks were touched with a reddish "blusher." Both men and women might be dressed in their everyday clothes, and given wigs and sandals to wear. Items of personal jewelry were placed on the body—and then it was ready to be wrapped in linen.

▷ **Waste disposal**
All used cloths, packing materials, natron bundles, and other mummification leftovers were wrapped in the shape of a person, called a *tekenu*. It was buried near the mummy's tomb, not in it.

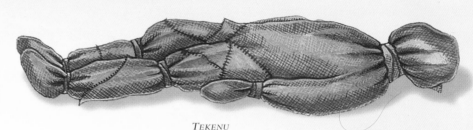

TEKENU

Protecting eye ▷
An Eye of Horus (*wedjat* eye) was put over the cut in the abdomen to stop evil entering the body.

A pharaoh's mummy usually had its arms crossed over its chest. Ordinary people were wrapped with their arms by their sides.

The embalming cut was rarely stitched up. Instead, it was covered with an Eye of Horus plaque.

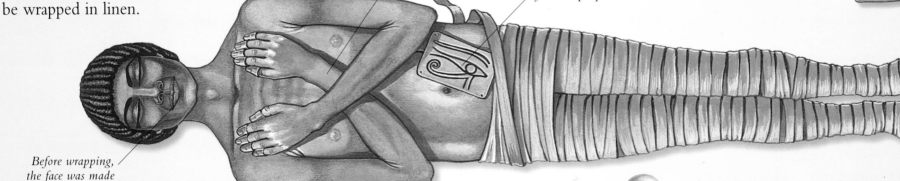

Before wrapping, the face was made to look as lifelike as possible.

FIFTEEN DAYS TO WRAP

It took fifteen days to wrap a body in strips and sheets of linen. Old clothes, bedsheets, and even ships' sails, were torn up and used. The head, fingers, toes, arms, and legs were wrapped first, then the torso. Wrappings then went around the whole body. Amulets and spells were placed between the layers. Resin was poured over the wrapped mummy to waterproof and strengthen it.

THE BODY BEAUTIFUL

Embalmers took great care to prepare the body before it was wrapped. They wanted it to look as much like a living body as possible, so its *ka* would recognize it. Besides a wig, clothes, and face makeup, balls of linen were pushed into the eye sockets and painted to look like real eyes. Some bodies had gold stalls (covers) placed over their fingers and toes.

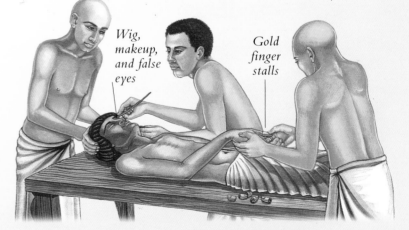

Wig, makeup, and false eyes

Gold finger stalls

BEAUTIFYING THE BODY

ORGAN CONTAINERS

The body's dried-out internal organs (lungs, stomach, liver, and intestines) were wrapped, then placed inside special containers. The containers, made from clay or stone, have come to be known as "canopic jars." They represented the Four Sons of Horus, and each one had a different head for a lid.

DUAMUTEF
(JACKAL)
STOMACH

QEBEHSENUEF
(FALCON)
INTESTINES

HAPI (BABOON)
LUNGS

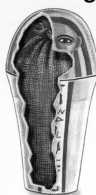

IMSETI (HUMAN)
LIVER

PAPYRUS COLUMN AMULET

HEART AMULET

HAND AMULET

WINGED SCARAB AMULET

△ **Amulets for protection**
Amulets, usually made from stone or glazed clay, were placed among the mummy wrappings. They were "lucky charms," whose job was to protect the person on the journey to the afterlife.

Amulets placed among the mummy's wrappings.

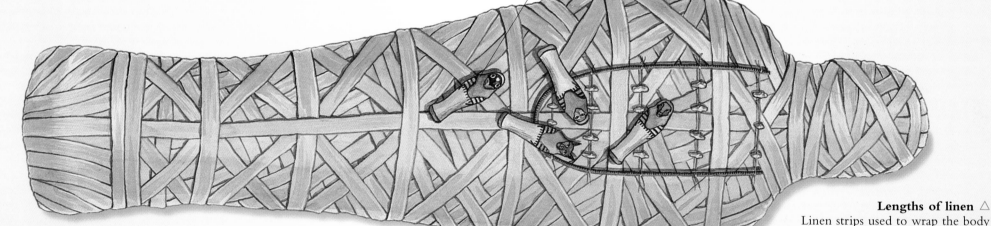

Lengths of linen △
Linen strips used to wrap the body were usually between 2½ and 8 inches (6 and 20 cm) in width.

THE WRAPPING STAGES

A huge quantity of linen was used to wrap even the humblest of bodies. It made the finished mummy seem quite bulky, while still retaining the basic outline of the body inside. The final wrapping was often a single large sheet of linen, which was held in place with linen bands. Sometimes the final wrapping was dyed red.

WRAPPED FOR ETERNITY

During the wrapping, priests chanted spells each time a new piece of linen was put in place. Like the amulets among the wrappings, the spells were also designed to protect the person's *akh*, helping it on its way to the next life where it would live again. When the wrapping was over, the body was no longer visible. It was then time to prepare for the funeral.

INTO THE COFFIN

The embalmers' last act was to place a mask over the head of the wrapped mummy. For most of Egyptian history, mummy masks were not true likenesses of the people they adorned. Instead, a mask was a way of showing how a person wanted to look in the next life. Once the mask had been fitted, the mummy was returned to its family, who took it across the Nile River, back to the person's home.

THE "CHEST OF LIFE"

A coffin, which the Egyptians called a "chest of life," was another form of protection for the mummy. The dead person's family provided it. Simple coffins were rectangular boxes made from wooden planks. Elaborate "mummiform" coffins were shaped like the body inside. Some mummies had a "nest" of coffins, where several fitted one inside the other.

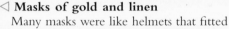

◁ **Masks of gold and linen**
Many masks were like helmets that fitted over a mummy's head and shoulders. Pharaohs' masks were usually of gold and semiprecious stones. Nobles' and commoners' masks were often made from cartonnage, which was linen stiffened with plaster and then painted.

Ready for its coffin ▽
The wrapped and masked mummy, protected by amulets, is now ready to be placed inside one or more coffins.

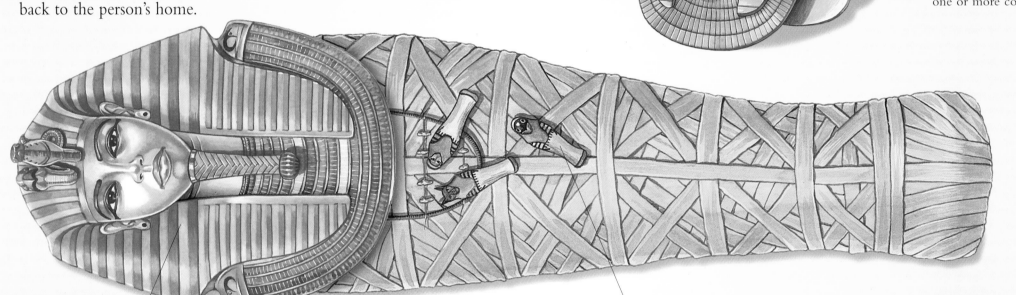

A gold mask on the mummy of a pharaoh. A mask helped the ba and ka recognize the person they were to serve.

▷ **In the round**
From the side, the rounded shape of a fully wrapped and masked mummy can easily be seen.

Spells from the Book of the Dead were inscribed on amulets and papyrus scrolls and placed among the mummy wrappings.

A VERY SAFE BOX

A coffin was a vital part of the business of ensuring that a person was reborn. It was like a "safe," whose purpose was to protect valuable contents. It was usually decorated on the outside and inside. Interiors were painted with protective spells, objects the person would need in the next life, and also a "map" that showed the route to the afterlife.

STONE FLESH EATER

While the embalmers worked to transform a body into a mummy, other groups of workers put the finishing touches to its tomb. If the dead person was from a royal or wealthy family, a stone sarcophagus might be made for the burial chamber. The coffin went inside it. "Sarcophagus" is from a Greek word meaning "flesh eater."

A sarcophagus was a container designed to protect a body.

△ **Stonemasons at work**
Stone was shaped with hammerstones, and chisels of copper and bronze.

STONEMASON'S TOOL

The coffin of a pharaoh showed the ruler holding two of the emblems of kingship—a crook-shaped scepter and a flail.

A COFFIN'S MEANING

In its most elaborate form, an Egyptian coffin was thought of as a miniature version of the universe. The lid, which often had stars painted on its underside, represented the sky, and the bottom part, where the mummy was, represented the Earth. When a mummy was inside its coffin, it was as if it had become a part of the universe itself. The Egyptians believed a person traveled from Earth to sky to live "among the imperishable stars."

The outer coffin ▽
The outer coffin containing the mummified body of a pharaoh. Made from wood, its surface was highly decorated.

◁ **Body-shaped coffin**
Perhaps the Egyptians thought a body-shaped coffin would act as a "substitute" for the real body, if that was destroyed. If so, then it was another way of helping a person reach the next life.

MUMMY MATTERS

👁 **Some Egyptian coffin facts**

• The Egyptians had two words for a coffin—*suhet* and *qersu*.
• Some mummies lay on their left sides inside their coffins, and were able to "see" out through eyes painted on the coffin sides.

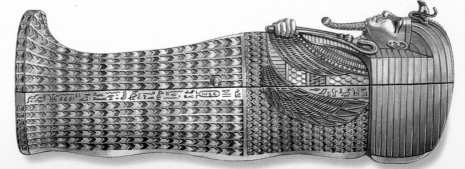

THE MUMMY'S TOMB

The day of burial was when a person began the journey into the next life. The work of the embalmers during the seventy days taken to make the mummy had prepared the person for this great moment in their "life." The final act was the placing of the mummy inside a tomb. The tomb was the ultimate body protector, where it was hoped the mummy would rest undisturbed forever. It would be attended by the *ba* and the *ka*, and the person would become immortal—an *akh*.

ON THE DAY OF BURIAL

At the person's house, the family put the mummy, in its coffin, onto a sled. Then, the funeral procession crossed the Nile River and headed to a cemetery. Many mourners walked with the sled. Some were family members, others were mourners whose job was to beat their chests, pull their hair, and wail aloud. Priests sprinkled milk, and burned sweet-smelling incense.

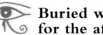

MUMMY MATTERS

Buried with goods for the afterlife

- Every Egyptian, from peasant to pharaoh, was buried with goods to use in the afterlife.
- Material goods were essential if the dead person was to live again.
- All dead people were buried with the most important grave goods of all—food and drink.
- Some were buried with everything they might need, from furniture to clothes, weapons to cosmetics, jewelry to musical instruments.

OPENING THE MOUTH

Outside the tomb, the mummy was taken from the coffin and stood upright. A *sem*-priest used a Y-shaped stone called a *pesesh-kef* to touch the mummy's mouth, eyes, ears, and nose. This act, known as the Opening of the Mouth ceremony, was to restore the person's senses.

▷ **A rock-cut tomb**
Pharaohs of the New Kingdom were buried in tombs cut into the rockface of a valley.

Sem-priest restoring a person's senses, so that he or she will be able to eat, drink, hear, see, and smell in the afterlife.

A chest holding the four canopic jars was carried separately.

A muu *dancer performed a ritual dance on the way to the tomb.*

TOMB ROBBERS AT WORK

After the burial ceremony was over, the entrance to the tomb was closed. In many cases, the entrance was then covered over with stones and sand. This was done to hide it from sight, in the hope that tomb robbers would not find it. Unfortunately, many tombs were broken into, often not long after they had been closed. Robbers entered tombs to steal anything they could use or sell. They had little care for the mummy, and ripped open its wrappings in their search.

TOMB TYPES

Egypt's first purpose-built tombs appeared around 3100 BCE, known as *mastaba* tombs, from an Arabic word meaning "bench." Built from clay bricks, they had a burial chamber under the ground. Around 2650 BCE, the first pyramid tomb was built. Pyramids were built as pharaohs' tombs, but their design failed to keep out raiders. From 1550 BCE, to defeat tomb robbers, pharaohs were buried in rock-cut tombs instead of pyramids.

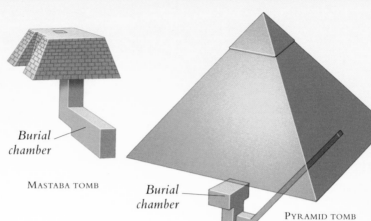

Burial chamber

MASTABA TOMB

Burial chamber

PYRAMID TOMB

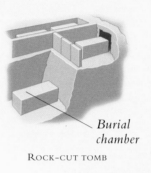

Burial chamber

ROCK-CUT TOMB

HELPED BY SERVANTS

As well as being buried with goods for the afterlife, a dead person was often provided with "servants," whose job was to help them when they got there. One of the joys of being reborn was never having to work again. Servants took the form of carved models, showing people doing everyday jobs, such as baking bread or tending to animals, or *shabti* ("answerer") figures. A person could be buried with hundreds of *shabti* figures.

SHABTI FIGURE

MODEL GRINDING CORN

◁ **Disturbing the dead**
Robbers took valuables, but left mummies in their tombs. Mummies whose tombs were disturbed were sometimes reburied, often in groups with others whose sleep had been disturbed.

MODEL WORKING
ON THE LAND

JOURNEY TO THE AFTERLIFE

Only when the mummy was sealed inside its tomb did the dead person begin the journey to the afterlife. On the journey, the person entered the Hall of Two Truths, where the Weighing of the Heart ceremony took place. The person was presented to a panel of forty-two judges, who accused him or her of crimes. The person denied them all. Then, their heart was weighed against a feather, to see if they had been truthful. If they had, the scales balanced, and they were allowed to enter the afterlife. If the heart was heavy with sin, it was eaten by a monster, and the person was condemned to a life of torment, never to enter the next life.

HELPFUL OR HARMFUL?

Once a person entered the afterlife, he or she was able to use supernatural powers. These powers could be put to good use, helping to solve problems for the living. However, they could also harm the living, causing them illness and trouble in the form of curses. One way of defeating a curse was to remove the person's name from their tomb, and damage their images. It was a way of destroying the individual.

Judges in the Hall of Two Truths. The dead person (far left) answers questions before his heart is weighed.

A person who passed the test was presented to Osiris, and was allowed to enter the afterlife.

Osiris, god of the afterlife, welcoming the dead person into the afterlife.

Isis and her sister, Nephthys, watched the judgement.

The dead person is led into the Hall of Two Truths by Anubis.

The person's heart on the scales.

Anubis adjusting the scales.

Ammut, waiting to eat the heart if the person fails the test.

The feather of truth against which the heart was weighed.

If a person passed the test, the god Thoth wrote that they were "true of voice."

Horus, presenting the dead person to Osiris.

Weighing of the heart △
In a scene from the Book of the Dead, a person is judged in the Hall of Two Truths. Will he enter the afterlife, or be condemned to a second death?

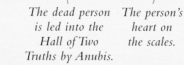

△ **Lucky charm**
Wrapped with the mummy was a heart scarab, on the underside of which was a protective spell from the Book of the Dead.

MAGIC HEART

Some particularly powerful spells from the Book of the Dead were written onto amulets. For example, amulets known as "heart scarabs," which were made to look like scarab beetles, were inscribed with a spell designed to stop a dead person's heart from speaking out against him or her during the Weighing of the Heart ceremony. The spell said:

O my heart which I had from my mother!
O my heart which I had from my mother!
O my heart of my different ages!
Do not stand up as a witness against me,
Do not be opposed to me in this tribunal,
Do not be hostile to me in the presence of the
Keeper of the Balance.

▷ **A second death**
The prospect of dying for a second time filled Egyptians with horror. It was the worst thing that could possibly happen to them.

DEVOURER OF THE DEAD

Ammut was a female monster thought to live in the underworld. She was portrayed as a creature with the head of a crocodile, the front of a lion, and the rear of a hippopotamus, each of which was a ferocious animal in its own right. Ammut was called the "devourer of the dead" because she ate the hearts of those who had led wicked lives. She was feared by all, and everyone knew that once she had eaten a person's heart, they could never reach the afterlife.

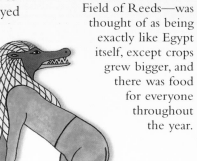
AMMUT

Home from home ▷
The afterlife—the Field of Reeds—was thought of as being exactly like Egypt itself, except crops grew bigger, and there was food for everyone throughout the year.

THE TORMENTED DEAD

For those unlucky enough to have their hearts eaten by Ammut, a terrible fate awaited them. If this happened, Egyptians believed they could not look forward to being reborn in the afterlife; they would not live in the Field of Reeds; they would not dwell "among the imperishable stars"; they would not become immortal. These people were sentenced to die a second time.
A "second dead" person faced eternal torment, and was punished in terrible ways, such as decapitation and being thrown onto fires. The person ceased to exist.

▷ **Meet the gods**
In the Hall of Two Truths, a dead person met the gods Horus and Thoth. Horus, who was the son of Osiris, was the god of eternal life. Thoth was the god of wisdom and writing.

HORUS   THOTH

DISCOVERING EGYPT

The magnificent civilization of ancient Egypt today casts a spell over people's imaginations. Visitors marvel at the ruins of its temples and pyramids, and look in wonder at objects in museums. As archeologists uncover and understand more of ancient Egypt's secrets, it is as if the past itself has been reborn, to live again in the present day. The ancient Egyptians wanted to live forever, and because we want to know about them, we are keeping their memory, and their legacy, alive.

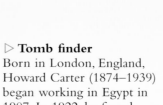

▷ **Tomb finder**
Born in London, England, Howard Carter (1874–1939) began working in Egypt in 1907. In 1922, he found the almost undisturbed tomb of the pharaoh Tutankhamun.

"WONDERFUL THINGS"
Howard Carter spent several seasons working in the Valley of the Kings, the burial ground of Egypt's New Kingdom pharaohs. On November 4, 1922, a stone step was found—the first in a staircase that led down to a sealed doorway, beyond which was a second door. On November 27, Carter made a hole in this door, and peered through. He said he could see "wonderful things."

TUTANKHAMUN

THE BOY KING
Tutankhamun became Egypt's pharaoh when he was nine years old, in 1336 BCE. He married Ankhesenamun, his half-sister. He was too young to rule on his own, and was helped by his ministers. He died aged eighteen, in 1327 BCE. Some people think he was murdered.

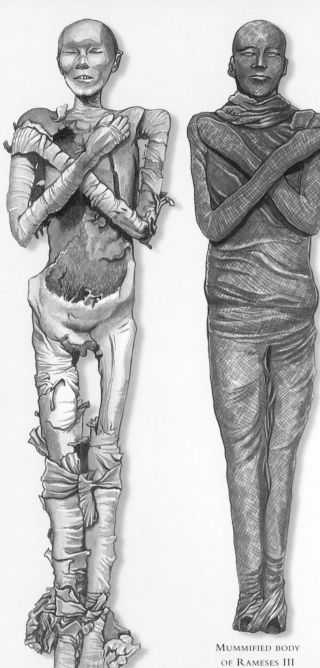

MUMMIFIED BODY
OF TUTHMOSIS II

MUMMIFIED BODY
OF RAMESES III

△ **Distant lives**
Some 3,500 years ago, these men lived on Earth as god-kings (pharoahs) of Egypt.

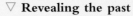 ▽ **Revealing the past**
A mummy enters a computerized axial tomography (CAT) scanner, in a hospital. This high-tech machine takes pictures of the body inside the wrappings.

Pictures taken by a CAT scanner reveal a body's soft tissue, whereas X-rays show its bones.

EXAMINING A MUMMY

A great amount of information can be learned by examining a mummy. Many mummies have been unwrapped, though nowadays this is rarely done, since there are ways of "seeing" inside the mummy without interfering with it, such as X-rays and body-scans.

ANIMAL MUMMIES

It wasn't only people that the Egyptians mummified. Cats, dogs, cows, fish, and many other animals, were embalmed. Some may have been favorite pets. Most were probably intended as food for the dead person in the afterlife.

THE THINGS WE LEARN

A mummy can tell us about the illnesses and diseases a person had, which are much like the ones people still suffer from today. Arthritis, a painful condition of the bone joints, and tuberculosis, a lung disease, have been found in mummies, as have signs of broken bones and amputated limbs. A mummy also reveals information about a person's diet. For example, worn-down teeth are a sign that a person ate food with grit in it, such as sandy bread—the wind blew sand into the dough at the bakery. Facts about the mummification process also come to light, telling how it changed over time. You can think of a mummy as an ancient Egyptian time capsule.

MUMMY MATTERS

 What they did with mummies

- In the 1800s, mummified cats were shipped to Liverpool, England, and were ground up for farm fertilizer.
- Powdered human mummies were made into "Mummy Brown," a pigment which artists used in their paintings.
- Mummies were used in medicines, and were said to cure all things, from coughs to broken bones.
- It's said that mummy arms and legs were used as torches at night.

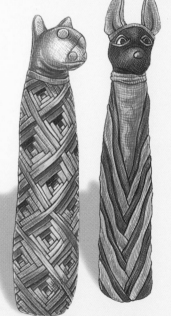

MUMMIFIED CAT AND DOG

GLOSSARY AND INDEX

afterlife The idea that after a person dies, a part of them continues to exist in a new life after death.

akh One of the "parts" of a person's identity. It formed when the *ba* and the *ka* joined together, and was the state in which the dead person existed in the afterlife as an immortal being. Pictured as a crested ibis bird.

Ammut Goddess who ate the hearts of people not allowed into the afterlife. She was the "devourer of the dead."

amulet An object used as a protective device or "lucky charm," to ward off evil.

Anubis God of embalming.

ba One of the "parts" of a person's identity. Usually described as their personality or character. It was freed from the body at death. Pictured as a human-headed bird.

Book of the Dead Collection of about 200 spells designed to protect the dead person and help him or her reach the afterlife.

canopic jars Four jars that held the mummified stomach, liver, lungs, and intestines of a person.

cartonnage Linen stiffened with plaster, used to make mummy masks and coffins.

embalmer A person who preserves the dead body of a person or an animal, so that it will not rot.

Horus God of the sky and eternal life, keeper of order. Son of Osiris and Isis.

ibu The "Place of Purification." An embalmers' tent where a body was cleansed before being mummified.

Isis Goddess of fertility and nature. Wife and sister of Osiris. Mother of Horus.

ka One of the "parts" of a person's identity. Usually described as their life force or "identical twin." Formed at birth and freed from the body at death, it lived in the person's tomb, where it was nourished by offerings left there for it. Pictured as a pair of upstretched arms.

lector priest A priest who recited the words of an Egyptian god at ceremonies and funerals. Wore a broad white sash across his chest.

mastaba A rectangular, bench-shaped tomb of mud-brick with a flat roof.

Master of Secrets The chief embalmer.

muu dancer A male dancer who performed at a funeral. Wore a kilt, and a tall hat made of reeds.

natron A type of salt gathered from the edges of lakes. Used by embalmers to dry out a body.

necropolis A cemetery. Means "city of the dead."

Nephthys Goddess who protected the dead. Wife of Seth, sister of Isis.

neteryt The name the Egyptians gave to natron.

obsidian A type of hard, shiny, glasslike stone.

Osiris God of the afterlife, and the dead. Husband and brother of Isis. Father of Horus.

per-nefer The "House of Beauty." An embalmers' tent where a body was mummified.

pesesh-kef A Y-shaped stone used to restore a person's senses at the Opening of the Mouth ceremony.

Ra God of creation, father of the gods. He was the sun god, and was the most important deity.

sarcophagus Stone container into which a coffin or a mummy was placed. Means "flesh eater."

scarab Dung beetle, associated with rebirth.

scribe A person trained to read and write.

sem-priest A priest, dressed in a leopard-skin garment, who officiated at a funeral, especially the Opening of the Mouth ceremony.

Seth God of chaos, storms, and evil. Husband of Nephthys, brother of Osiris and Isis.

shabti Wooden or glazed clay figure. Worked as a servant for the dead person in the afterlife.

tekenu A bundle formed from linen wads, used natron, and so on, which had been used in the mummification process and which had come into contact with the body. Buried outside the tomb.

Thoth God of wisdom, writing, reading, magic, and mathematics.

wedjat eye The left eye of Horus. It symbolized the power of healing and was a powerful amulet.